The Turning Sky

The Turning Sky

by Sydney Tremayne

Rupert Hart-Davis LONDON 1969

© Sydney Tremayne 1969
First published 1969
Rupert Hart-Davis Ltd
3 Upper James Street,
Golden Square, London W1

Printed in Great Britain by
The Bowering Press, Plymouth

SBN: 246 97440 0

Acknowledgments

Some of these poems were first published in the Listener,
New Statesman, Spectator, Scottish Field, Scottish
Poetry Nos. 1, 2 and 3 (Edinburgh University Press),
Modern Scottish Poetry (Faber), A Book of Scottish
Verse (OUP World's Classics series), The Scottish
Literary Revival (Collier-Macmillan), Commonwealth
Poems of Today (John Murray for the English
Association), PEN New Poems 1965, Lines, the Poetry
Review, English, the Yorkshire Post, Orient-West,
Tokyo, and Poet, Madras. Acknowledgment is made
to the editors, also to the BBC Scottish and Third
Programmes.

Contents

Contents

Lethe

All woulds and shoulds and mights are cancelled out,
Nothing exists that once moved in her head,
Days, nights, the faces of her sons (not dead
But as unborn, undreamed of); no regret
For what was done, or lost, or can't become,
The green leaves gone, broken companionship;
Unwound from clinging webs that trammel sleep
She neither dreams nor wakens. Then for whom,
Except ourselves, this outcry at her death?
Ourselves are wounded, since she can forget
Even this air and all our shared daylight
Though we protest our love to our last breath.

North of Berwick

Slowly the sea is parted from the sky:
The light surprises, crinkling on the water.
The white sun hardens; cliffs solidify.
A long coast of red rock where three swans fly
Engraves itself in calm, deceptive weather.

Three swans fly north, a diesel thumping south
Draws out of sight along the rusting railway,
All windows clouded with a communal breath.
Fields flash in the sunlight, far beneath
The sea turns in its scales, well in a seal's way.

No boat invades that shining emptiness.
Because the waves are distant, the sky windless,
That pale line round the shore looks motionless.
Hearing such border warfare lost in space
You say the breathing of the sea is endless.

What is the one thing constant? Can you say?
The loneliness that we are born to merges
Perhaps with such a place on such a day.
No stones cry out because we cannot stay.
Through all our absences the long tide surges.

A Sign of Permanence

Descending the Heads of Ayr on an autumn morning
The sea gunmetal, pale the uncut barley,
Shy as a man from jail avoiding parley
Lightly he looked in where the great sky turning
Deployed its gulls gliding from cloud to cloud,
His oldest images, an idle crowd.

Fished from the air, from nowhere, from a vision
Long frozen under silence, rocks grew solid.
In this awakened vision the waves volleyed
Over the rocks, collision and erosion
Rhythmical ground bass to the choral wind
Vibrating up the needle of his mind.

An old head back among its windy spaces
He searched the sand most studiously for nothing,
Picked up a stone and kept it for a plaything,
Noted the low trees twisted in their places
By the prevailing wind they could not miss
And felt a sense of permanence in this.

Burrow Head

Bullocks and sheep unsafely graze
On high cliffs shrouded in sea haze.
Four shags ride an upward wind,
On stiff wings planing briskly round.
A pair of kestrels hang and drop,
Quartering a naked slope.
Abandoned gun sites, broken huts
Rot peacefully, like worked-out pits.
The grey sky crawls on the grey sea:
Each ninety seconds, night and day,
A far-off foghorn sounds its groan.
Nothing replies, and yet again
The man-made warning's monstrous voice
Calls out into emptiness.
Let us sit among the rocks
And count how long the silence takes,
Watch the kestrels drop and rise,
Tireless birds with downward eyes.
Inch by inch the kestrels' stare
Strips the grassy hillside bare
And the tide moves up and down
From one stone to another stone.

The World as a Perpetual Fire

Sunlight like shoals of phosphorescent fish
Leaps from the water pizzicato. Heat
Smacks on the rocks; white flecks of mica flash
Stranded among the hillside's dusty peat,
Brilliant as minnows floundering in a net.

Flat loch and sky are cymbals, ringing brass,
Stones dancing atoms; rhododendrons tear
The heavy air with colour, leaves of glass
Multiply light, making a blinding flare
Round every burning bush by the still shore.

Did the eyes thirst for clarity? More light
Splinters the world to a percussive blaze.
A dot no bigger than a fly, a boat
Out there between the simmering islands, goes
Into a light that drowns it from our gaze.

Sinking in bracken, sheltered among fronds,
Stretched out like wool, the witless body lies
Grounded upon a shadow. At those bounds
The scintillating rage of sunlight dies
To distant sounds, scarce audible gull cries.

Upon a warm skin and a vacant mind
More daylight pours than eyes for long can bear.
Merged with the lizard world, we have attained
For once that liberation from desire
The next breath startles back from, a green snare.

Staccato trumpets of the sun proclaim
The world on fire above if not below.
Hairs glow like tapers, fiery beetles climb
Up scorching grass to search the source and flow
Of cloudless light, perpetual or no.

Earth Spirits

The leveret in the leaves
Eating forget-me-nots freshly in bloom,
Pulling the heads off and reversing them
Fastidiously, thrives;
Also the weasel thrives, the sleek rat thrives
In this great time of plenty that arrives.

The world of the young hare
Is hairy as his milky mother's teat
Who suckles him and rolls him off his feet,
Licks him with rapid care,
Then leaves him with a leap to his own care
Among forget-me-nots to sit and stare.

Staring through sunlit hours
As in a dream, his harebrained vision flies
Over the fields, alert how the land lies
Outside the bed of flowers.
Not to be found but find, for instance, flowers
Is fortune in this Eden set with snares.

Colour of earth, alone
Almost from birth, hares when they reach full size
Leer out of landscapes like sardonic spies,
Hares that are closer kin
To tuft and stone than to their nearest kin,
And hold their ground by knowing where to run.

Discomfort in High Places

Slopping like sphagnum, battered, baptised in cloud,
A leak in every crevice of the soul,
Bones would be warmer bundled in a hole:
White rainstorms beat the mountain's barren head.

Moses was not hauled high on such a day.
All beasts go down, the ravens dive from sight
When the skies open and the floods fall out
And hills are busy sweeping themselves away.

Mist hides the edge of nowhere, which is close.
Miss a short step, and the skied body's fall
Flips a few stones that drop like a burst shell.
Through steaming gullies burns jump the rockface.

Below the mist, down by the salt loch shore
A white rose streams at the end of a wild stalk.
Wind clouts shut doors. What news is there to hawk
Of turbulence, water and everlasting air?

The Captives

A close community of two:
Outside, a storm bangs like the police.
Arrest the world; it will not do
To breach this consummated peace.

Two conscripts, man and woman, free
At last to choose a place to sleep,
Who cannot sleep, have turned the key
And don't lie weary counting sheep.

These two now serve as volunteers,
Comrades in arms, and it is right,
Lest they are dead meat in the snares
That freedom's partisans unite.

Two captives loosed by an exchange
Reveal the heart of liberty:
Nothing that politics arrange,
But choosing a captivity.

A Sense of Balance

Riding, erect and solemn, his twenty-six-year-old bicycle,
Spats revolving in slow motion with the rat trap pedals,
Our father, bearing his ample umbrella perpendicular,
Ruled on the rainy road a wake of comparative dryness
As he moved in his dignity through the slate roofed town.

Story for Imperialists

My father's father's sword, hung on the wall,
Was blunt in fact and ceremonial.
I'd borrow it in secret, draw it out,
Lunge at a tree with full five stone of weight,
Watch the blade curve and whip back straight.
Nothing I tried could even burr the point.
I claimed its virtues, growing confident,
Squinting with narrow exaltation, rather
As though to close one eye to fact and father.
Yet my small son has snapped this blade in half
Like a dry stick, a rotten staff,
Not in romantic emulation,
But digging worms with Freudian fascination.
The hilt lies in my hand. A broken blade,
Appropriate enough, leads no crusade
And in a dustbin shall be laid,
False prop of the imagination's games,
Burdened with father's father's father's names.

Slump

It wasn't pride but funk, a shallow failure.
I should have joined the dole queue but could not,
Could hardly stand there weeping in the street
Making a common accident peculiar,
So sloped away, confused, and kept apart
Fencing those victims from my fancy heart.

Nineteen years old, self-centred and romantic,
It was of course a privilege that I claimed
Not to show up, not to be openly named
One of the luckless faces, those authentic
Masses that one might pity from afar
Rather like conscripts in a hopeless war.

Lived for a month on lentil soup and porridge,
Deceived the landlord with an affluent air
(Fur gloves, an ebony stick, a cheap cigar:
A taste that some might privately disparage).
It seems I must have wished to look distinguished,
Making a shine because eclipse was anguished.

This should be rounded primly with a moral.
The sufferings of hurt vanity are gross.
The common lot is never meant for us.
Poor fish, the king of herrings in a barrel
Is priced no better for his bonny scales.
Kippers are twins. Equality prevails.

A Night Fire Call

Dawn breaks and I discover myself
On top of a wall much higher than I imagined
Which is on top of a hill that I didn't know about.
Peering down over a drop of plummet precipitousness
I reflect that I have been strolling most of the night
On this wall about one foot wide flashing an axe,
Chopping the red bits out of smouldering timbers.
All of which is so like the world on its regular sleepwalk,
So much like the usual ignorant tightrope dance
On a half frayed tightrope over a hidden bearpit,
That I think the power of darkness is our salvation.
If I'd seen where I was I'd have broken my neck.

Magnetic Disturbance

Knowing that this was nonsense, knowing it well,
He was tormented by an electric girl.
Sparks crowned her head and glittered in her eyes
And like a searchlight pinned him in surprise.
Did he like her? Honestly no, honestly no.
Bed was the place he wanted her to go
And dreamed she did but always knew he dreamed,
And she, well pleased to be this way esteemed,
Switched on more voltage, negligently bright
As a celestial body's broadcast light.

Stone Walls

A calm house for a child.
Father and mother keep their separate rooms
On separate landings. No one comes.
The world outside goes wild,
Russia and Ireland stick with blood.
Here history is a book of naval battles
With wooden ships, chain shot and grapples,
Remote from now as Noah's flood.

Relics tell nothing plainly:
Bags of old golf clubs, fiddle, hipbath, cello,
Stacks of sheet music, dog-eared, turning yellow.
Come, come, I love you only . . .
Whose love was true? Wind sings
Soprano at the keyhole. It is cold
Outside and inside where the unpractised child
Plunks at the cello strings

Or moons from room to room
On a vague visit to familiars. Who,
Tuning the strings more brightly, drew,
Before the guns went boom,
Harmonies soon suppressed
For lack of listening to? What strenuous play
Do punchbag, dumb-bells, Indian clubs convey
Dumped in the attic dust?

The photographs are torn.
The unknown grandfather, bewhiskered, scowls
Beside a pistol and a box of pills
In magisterial scorn.

His framed glare stiffly stands
As a memento mori or a totem.
Here ends the Stone Age, after which no item
Escaped the censoring hands.

Past childwit to suppose
The young and frivolous parents playing house,
Waking an Eden in their warm embrace
Who cannot now compose
A plausible meeting face.
By this the first commandment is impressed:
Let the emotions keep their distance lest
The dumb-bells think disgrace.

Hundreds of miles apart
Those two lie now in dark that hides for good
The family skeletons, bridegroom and bride
In tune at the false start.
What am I bid for these
Starched collars, chopsticks, sea chest and spittoon?
Going, going, are you done, are you all done? Gone.
Somebody has a prize.

The deadness of the dead
Lengthens, for all the features haunting mirrors,
Type faces, sticking out like printers' errors,
That nose, that shape of head.
Quietness fills the house.
Sparrows chirp in the ivy. The child strums
Gems from Maritana. Nobody comes
To wake this world from peace.

The outer world's bemused.
The khaki unemployed have wounded faces.
Lord Lonsdale's yellow coach drives to the races.
In the asylum bruised
Cassandras locked up cry
While Hitler ripens slowly from decay.
In schools they hear of Bruce and Empire Day
And which way up flags fly.

Acock his rocking horse
The child rocks till the papered wall streams round.
Stone walls do not a fortress make that stand
Like scenery in a farce
Shaking if doors are tried.
Two songsters ill adapted to one cage
Sang here and brought a third upon the stage
Before the singing died.

A Father Thinks about His Son

Whether we'll meet again neither can guess:
You have to go and I must stay
And all the goodwill we possess
Send news between two worlds as best it may.

We'll have our images, though out of date,
Each of us pictured younger than
The years allow, a godlike state,
Writing of changes, you of those you plan.

Four generations blown before the wind,
A century of scattering, leaves
This thinned-out family like mankind:
Brothers and strangers, birds in foreign eaves.

To be in this world settled anywhere
Is rare good fortune, or seems so.
Close in the brambles sits the hare,
You go to find what fortune may bestow.

This too is good, to set out for new shores
Rid of all lumber, travelling light,
A later Lazarus who explores
A strange earth opening with new sight

And leaves behind him nothing but a death,
Second of many separations,
Birth being first, that gave him breath
And the wide air for his interrogations.

A Father Thinks about His Son

Born as we were beneath a different sky,
Twenty years longer in my head,
You run beyond my vision, fly
Out of this picture where I am delayed.

Yet minds are jumping jacks and sometimes leap
Not only space but distant time.
Now you and your young family keep
A presence in this house; I climb

At midnight to my look-out post and write
How the moon rises hard and clear
While all the fields lie glimmering white
And time seems motionless in the still air.

Mixed Weather

The holly leaves are glinting in the sun.
Thumped by the wind half senseless we come in,
Into our wits and out of part of our senses,
To watch how the light dances
And lie to ourselves that the long winter's done.

The naked trees roll wildly. Hedges lean
Ready to take off smartly from the scene.
Shadows, dead leaves and flurries of snow are flying,
All fixity's for denying
And wind blurts at the door like a trombone.

Forty-foot cherry trees lie on the ground
Roots raised like horns, no more to be earthbound.
The sky is blue and white and dark and glowing.
A rock in the tide's flowing
The hill is hit by wave upon wave of sound.

At last the sun goes down, an orange blaze,
And night takes over with a darker noise.
My collie dog who wags his tail in sleeping
Feels he is in safe keeping
Lacking the fearful forethought we call wise.

Lock the door, trusting that it won't blow in.
Hear how the world's alive. The haring moon
Breaks cover and goes tearing into space,
Space that is like packed ice
With all the furies yelling out of tune.

Trees in their Crowding

In the high woods the wind is swinging;
The rooks dive through it; they whirl away.
The sky stretched up from the south is bringing
A head of rain. On a worsening day

Alone and idle I watch time filling
That needs no killing, that is a tide
Swelling and falling at no man's willing.
The leaves dance and are blown aside.

Trees in their crowding clash, entangle,
Roots in the clay and no bough still.
The straight rain drives at a sharpened angle;
The wash of the wind curves to the hill.

The Hare

In the split woods a broken sapling,
Cold catkins that I stoop below.
Explosion of a blackbird's wings
Kicks up exclamatory snow.

Silence, the burden of the song,
Resumes where winds have blasted through.
The white fields swell to the dark sky,
The matrix they are frozen to.

Stopped in my fiftieth winter's track
I see the maze a March hare ran.
This wilderness supports a hare;
It also may support a man.

Frost

Blue and red sky and fields crusted with frost,
The air itself so frozen it won't move:
Feet bang hard ground that yesterday was paste
And not a stone will budge out of its groove.
The hilltop's isolated in clear space.
On coated grass, spiky as coral, fall
Retrieves of sun, splinters off lunar ice,
Sun shooting wide as day goes down the scale
Through red, through gradual yellow, dying out.
The rising of the night is now complete.
Nothing but time has stirred, the world reset
With no more movement than a change of light.
The magnitude of silence fixes here
The moon, the whitened roof, the leafless wood,
The crisp stars freezing with a greenish fire,
The hill beyond this hill, our solitude.

Outpost in Winter

Mist lines the ground, a tracing of fine snow.
The field's unsettled as a sea
Through which the moles like whales come up to blow.
The tree that swims in grey might be
A spineless weed buoyed up to reach the air.
Silence is deep. Night shrinks. There is no star.

We two adrift in winter share with birds
Confinement of the dark that comes,
Silence banked upon silence, stranding words.
Outside, unsleeping stillness thrums
To our intensive listening like a heart
Echoing back from depths not on the chart.

Something that needs a refuge scrapes the eaves,
Birdfoot or ratfoot stirs the straw.
There is no wind to move the fallen leaves
For we should hear it softly draw
Ripples along the darkness: nothing at all
Except what seeks the shelter of a wall.

This is the arc of winter bending through
Its longest circuit from the light,
And we among the creatures, few,
That have a stake here, riding out the night
Feel the slow shift of time like a great strength
Reaching us up against our tether's length.

Flight in the Dark

Straight forward seemed the only way to go.
Skidding and pushing at the glass
A blue tit bursting out of night
Fought with the treacherous skin of light.
Wild with the window that it couldn't pass
Its eyes and all its colours were aglow.

Maybe it woke and took this for sunrise.
Around it everything was black,
A nightmare nonexistence; thence
Straight forward leapt a ray of sense.
Once launched incapable of turning back
Small wit, great panic struck at sun's disguise.

Inside the room what could be done except
Turn out the light before the bird
Injured its featherweight of brain?
It vanished, no doubt sideways, then.
Too much illumination had obscured
The crevice where it settled, safe, and slept.

Night Drivers

Here on the hilltop not a leaf is stirring.
Far down the night the lights of traffic pass:
Attentive brains are steering behind glass,
Voyagers in glass cases sharing
Projectile isolation and a trust,
Implicit, in a mode of common caring,
Moving by rote else some bleed in the dust.

Over me, space and silence. Isolation.
I look up into night where a thin cloud
Filters the moonlight. Sharp the anchored wood
Whose twisted spars make mediation
Between unending distance and this ground
On which we move and fix our habitation
And learn the ties by which the heart is bound.

Invisible the drivers and the driven.
Two puny streams of light creep opposite ways,
Carnival dragons lit up to amaze
Small children who instead are given
Glimpse of a darker heaven. High and low
The searchers hunt to find a proven haven,
Dazzled or blacked out suddenly as they go.

Inevitability

Sun, pale tissue paper, cannot light
The mist that is a travesty of white.
The dark is coming soon without a day,
And this is not what I had meant to say.

No, I was thinking how I sell my time
As millions must, reasoning without rhyme,
How the queer labour that the world requires
Is poking ashes without lighting fires.

The sun is cold, caught in a standing cloud.
Nonsense. So high the clouds are not allowed
And no one there makes poems, for the heat.
There is more life to waste in every street.

O life, O sun, O nonsense, and O time.
When past the missing stairs like spores we climb
In such combustion we participate
As fires the rose to its determined state.

Moonlight

The landscape in the moonlight lies
Like a long cloud beneath a lighter sky.
Here is the instant when the refugees
Forget that each goes shadowed by a spy,
Absorbed beyond conclusions, stilled
Into a stillness that wants no reply.

Restricted too much or compelled,
Nowhere to turn, no hope to break away,
The spirit quietens and unfists its hold
Shaking no more the cell that has no key,
Then goes out simply, with no shield,
By the least gap, the opening of an eye.

Stillness and clarity attend
Upon one instant's inattentiveness
And are escape from nothing in the end
But the mind's cowering in a narrow space,
Man being a ghost that can't be chained.
Look, there is only moonlight in his place.

Hailstones

That this was I, that this was you
Nobody cares, none shall know.
Are we together in this place?
Vapour scattered into space.
Count no favour, fear no truth:
The stars burn black as a charred cloth,
Black the day, black the night,
Yet black is no more black than white.
Hailstones fell in a white stream,
The sun comes out, now they are steam.
If we are dreams clouds are not so.
About the earth crosswinds blow.

Torridon

Moving with care across the jagged scree
I see the road below me twist away
And overhead the peak shortens the sky
And, underneath, a blue car like a fly
Crawling along takes minutes to get clear.
The engine sound floats upward where the deer
About a mile off graze and steadily drift
Along a green ledge tilted to a cleft
Through the black rock: there water splashes down.
Steeply below, straight cliffs, then tumbled stone,
Then humps of yellowed sphagnum and rough grass
Sweep to the river burrowing through the pass.
Upward again emerge a rib of snow
And clouds that trace the ridge but let it go
Until it stands carved keen against the sun.
Suddenly stillness cracks like a fired gun
And a great clattering, pounding, shunting slide
Goes on and on, echoed from every side,
Then stops. Time tipped the balance of a stone:
The slip reverberates, the fall's unseen.
Currents of air, confusingly, by turns
Carry then cancel out the noise of burns
Clashing down rocks or rumbling underground.
Rare silence, an expectancy of sound,
Makes quick the animal senses. Cloud drifts white;
Hills beyond hills jut through the tumbled light.
Nearby, below me on a patch of green
Lies a starved sheep, its ribs laid bare and clean.
The scattered wool a pair of eagles plucked
Clings in the grass. I save a feather picked

Torridon

Out of the mass still soggy from past rain.
Nothing much lives here but the ptarmigan,
The eagles' food that hides in the high rocks.
The uninhabitable region takes
Whatever breaks, and breaks it without spite,
Drawing the mind whole into mindless height.

The High Corrie

The man hidden in this place had cold bones.
The loch is black, shadowed by cliffs that rise
Barely as organ pipes. Three sides enclose
A wide stone ledge littered with separate stones;
Over the fourth side dives a waterfall.
The wind leans in on that side like a wall.

And far below the dark wet country shelves,
Pocked with moraines and cratered with green bogs.
A hunted man need fear only the dogs
And yet I doubt the stones drew round like wolves.
Snow in the wind's stone teeth, the waterfall
Stiffening to sleep trails down like a lost shawl.

Elements and Adaptations

A rook climbs down the wind step after step
Yet overshoots the catapulting tree,
Takes the invisible escalator up
And sails in weightless orbit round the sky.

A trout flies in fast water, hovering
Firm as a kestrel in the pushing stream,
Vibrating tail, fins quick as a snake's tongue,
Tonnage of water rumbling like a drum.

Men in their gale of chances unforeseen,
Anchored by apparatus, tug and strain,
Also break out of nature's neat design
To pot the moon with a precise machine.

The Mole

Pig-bodied mole, I pull you out
Stiffened with rage from tail to snout
With rage and terror in the light
Wild to escape and wild to bite.

Your tail erect lends me the grip
By which like meat I swing you up.
Out of this lawn I'll have you gone.
Trot for your skin: your time's not done.

I am volcano, hurricane,
Too blind a fury to explain.
Yet we are like. In fury, go.
What grip comes down I do not know.

The Wooden House

Drowning in grass and dwarfed by aged trees
The wooden house inhabited by birds
Looks like a hiding place for refugees,
Train robbers maybe, sheltering behind beards
And cultivating bracken up to the chin.
These hidden paths are devious as sin.

From here what look-out's possible? A loop
Of rotten rope holds up the broken gate.
A tumbling mass of roses and a group
Of mossgrown apple trees proliferate
So near the windows they conceal the track
Those crooks must use to leave by or come back.

One may be listening closely as a hare
Or lurking behind brambles like a fox
Who carries loot and drops it, though with care,
And circles back, nosing the air for shocks
When confidence and night make the wood his
But for the house in dark parenthesis.

Then on the rooftop owls that hoot and hiss
Chill the rats' blood. Pierced by that siren wail
Rats' rustling stops at once, their kicked hearts race,
They cringe down where they are to make them small.
Starlings fluff out their feathers under the eaves,
Squatters awakened by alarm of thieves.

The house seems only shadow in the night.
The sleepers are surrounded but lie low,
Light sleepers, having no need of a light
To read the signs around them, or to show
The world of prey a target it may miss
Following false trails in a wilderness.

Mouse

Fieldmouse absurdly small
Climbing up the wall
You have survived this week
Because your moves are quick
Yet you rampage around
With a rumbustious sound
Toppling glasses, jumping,
Tearing paper, thumping
Like a poltergeist
Until we are enticed
Into a daft pursuit
Useless as a flea shoot;
Must you be such a twerp
As sit around and chirp
Fixing a candid eye
On monsters standing by
As if they were extinct?
Your life with ours is linked
Because you thought it good
To join our solitude
And danced in the dog's face
With Salomé's wild grace
Until his eyes were crossed
And sense of direction lost.
Yet need you hoof so loud
That one mouse seems a crowd,
A cupboard full of feet?
Small fry should be discreet.
Small irritations make
A world their bailiwick

And dominate all sense
Till blood pays for offence.
Profit from this advice
And be as quiet as mice.

For C without Exaggeration

Seagull chicks on the rocks
A sun twice normal size
The sea shooting off sparks
And a poet shooting off lies.

In the light edging the land
Where seals popped up like souls
It was you they rose to find,
Then applauding with their tails

Followed from bay to bay
Splashing to make you look,
More vivid, dexterous, gay
Than words stiffened into a book.

Truly there's not a word
Can celebrate as I wish
Beauty by seals preferred
To a shoal of shining fish.

That such perfections live
The rocks are there to prove.
Plain facts are all I give
And of course my love, my love.

The Turning Sky

Sky in slow motion
The wide vacant sands
Arran across the sea
Great spaciousness
Clear light, keen wind
The summer ending,
White peaks to the waves,
Horizon curving,
Space to be lost in,
Yet not lost,
A visitor where
I learned to speak,
Quiescent as
The sandgrains blowing
I drift and listen
To the drift
Of the sea breaking
And the creaking
Eternal, unoriginal
Talk of the gulls.
Today I drove
Past the sold house
Where if I could
I would not live.
It was awake,
Inhabited.
By the Doonfoot
As always thrive
The marguerites
That first I saw

The Turning Sky

Half a century ago.
A swan preens
For its photograph
In the calm stream
With civil grace
That nothing
So expected
Be absent
From its place.
Three boys fishing
Catch nothing
Caught in the great light
Of the turning sky.

Untrampled Sand

In the brass light of morning, fire along the grass,
The tide far out, turning, the wind at peace,
The vivid sky stood open, a scene with nothing wrong:
Sun was sun, stones were stones, colours sharp and strong.
The gasworks and the barracks and the red Victorian jail
Were accepted in the pattern: a child's world well.

White in the height of morning the cenotaph was new.
The town lay sleeping like the dead: dead I didn't know.
The first light was created: on the untrampled sand
The curved salt lines extended like an unread hand.
There is a shining of the mind that takes its light from there.
White names on the cenotaph. Children grown to war.

Landmarks

Mist floods the valley under the moon
And forms a landlocked sea,
The long hillcrest pared to a line
Is a dark shore with lights that shine
The far side of a bay.
What is known and what is shown
At variance though they be,
When vanished tides start back again
They move the ground away.

Who would expect the hills to shrink
To the level of the sea,
Or sea to rise up to the brink
Where solid hills were used to drink
Lipping the flowing sky,
Or that sky blandly would unthink
All that the blinkered eye
Tutored by plain words in black ink
Agreed to reason by?

The ghost of water shapes no sound
Around the absent shore
That maps ignore with single mind;
No one may doubt them, yet I stand
In two worlds at my door.
Whether the wind tears up the sand
Or cannot shift a hair,
The groundswell that defines the ground
Insistently is there.

All voices have a different tone,
Those who know them know.
Worlds that were apart combine,
Voices do not come again,
Voices cease and go
Leaving silence like the moon
To settle in and grow,
Worn-out words on an old stone
With nothing more to show.

The Municipal Cemetery

The tombstones march, claiming another field.
Green April glutted by the rain is filled
With daffodils unfolding yellow light.
Vans in the railway siding, dusty white,
Are labelled Interfrigo. Square false teeth,
The rigid grin of headstones makes uncouth
Advertisement of bones. The broad land climbs
To a long skyline, burdened. All those names
Chiselled on standard slabs, solemnified,
Entered on numbered plans, admission paid,
Are laid out in their neighbourhoods like towns,
Which seems a waste, for under their private stones
The citizens disappear from this bogus place,
Who's Who of many names minus a face.

The April rain, not bogus, soaks the ground,
Corrupts no one; falling on sea and land
Is salted, mixed with sap or dust of streets,
Explores all forms, keeps none, evaporates
As if it had been bogus after all.
Who sits up there counting the heads that fall,
Keeping the register? Whatever you want, we stock it.
Replacement eye socket? Certainly. Sign the docket.
Collect now, pay later under our easy plan.
Most parts available except, so far, a new brain.

Light filters through these mass reduction lines,
Through gravestones in cab ranks, in traffic lanes
Jammed tight as if to meet some public boast,
The ordered city, or the multiple ghost.
Forests of pious periscopes are stuck

Out of the ground like chimneys without smoke.
It seems that death's inflation beggars all.
One thinks of overspill and overkill
And Interfrigo's trademark on the vans,
Cargoes that have been carried locked in trains
On mass migrations of these recent times:
A sense of vacuous industry overwhelms
Whatever sermons should collect in stones
Uniform as the civic rubbish bins.
A fine and public place is this, although
New as the trees that need more time to grow.
Here families tramp on Sundays, for whom wait
Hawkers with flowers in baskets at the gate.

Let the dead go. Forget them decently,
Spent breath in a live wind that absently
Resumes them to itself. If every breath
Bred its due monolith, stones of our youth
Would block the lungs' blind alleys. There's no dam
To stem the drift of time that would not maim
The fishy infant swimming to be born
And stranded on the rocks. Self love, forlorn
In all its tricks, has blown up death too high
Because it cannot bear that love should die.
Our mongrel ancestry thrives in our veins:
In this white place of regulation stones
Nothing to care for, nothing that cares who cares,
As dead to April rain as Auschwitz fires.

Details from a Death Certificate

The night is loud with aircraft noises.
A shadow like a mountain barrier rises
But is in truth the edge of the dark wood
Rigid and silent when the wind is dead,
As now it is, except that aeroplanes
Call back the howling sirens and the grains
Trickling from broken sandbags. Spilled like sand
Towns are built up again. Barricades of the mind
Screen us against each other as we demand
Till death us part; always the barriers stand.

No use pretending they could bear each other,
Either the rootless son or the racked father
With the raw pustulence weeping through his skin
From the frustration he was burning in.
Dead for nine years before his death was known,
Of cancer, in a wartime hospital.
Where are his bones? Who gave him burial?
God knows. I guess. War had no time for Lear.
In Auschwitz, Dresden, Coventry thousands more
Were lost, not to be heard of anywhere.

In the stark wood a blinded creature crawls
Who was a king among the nursery dolls
And with his daughter in his arms ran crying
Because he had a dream that she was dying
But later turned on her, harsh to appeals.
I will lift up my eyes to the bare hills
From whence can come no help, and find a grace
In thinking how the centuries pass

In the high air, however cold and wild,
Far from the human frenzy that has killed
More cruelly than time has wit;
Because the mind must rise from its black state
Knowing each life that has been or will be
Only a flash of leaves upon a tree
And light that pierces the dark wood
The one incomparable good:
Some instant of responsive sight
Unscreened like a wide sea of moving light.

It is the human desert that appals,
Each relic rotting like a tree that falls
Slowly to powder, dropping piece by piece,
Separate in that hideous hiding place
Where the hysterias sprout from the dead ground
And bloat upon the stumps littered around
And words aimed into dark communicate
No better than dogs that bark across the night.

These details from his death certificate:
Under the anaesthetic the heart's beat
Stopped and did not restart. To search out more
Would profit no one. Let that door
Be closed as it was closed before.

At first, some choice, so little in the end.
We cannot help each other much. I find
The menace of the world too close, and know
If courage goes everything else must go

And am afraid of that more than all else,
Even though courage frequently is false,
Like children in the dark sweating with fear
Not crying out because a creaking stair
Brings trust that they are watched on earth,
Safe by the fortune of their birth.

The vision that a man is quietened by
May hold a childish world: an empty sky
Above the morning hills, the coloured sea
Rocking the light and scattering spray,
Or in the harbour hulls of boats reflecting
The running light that the sea keeps projecting,
But never his own face there nor any face,
Nothing of yesterday or times that pass,
Only the moving light and the waves rolling
Without meaning, without ceasing, without consoling.

This man was small, nautical, musical,
Who in his world, albeit marginal,
Might curiously dream
Before the ruin of his self esteem
Cracked his life open like a broken ship
And flung him to the water's killing grip,
A foundered father fathoms down:
These pictures shirk that struggling and that pain.

The barriers stand. The planes fly out of sight.
No searchlights follow them. The fires are out
That changed the streets. Elsewhere, in Asia, still
The frightened killers kill and the bombs fall,

Details from a Death Certificate

And at the Berlin Wall murder is done
To bend life to an artificial line.
The banished men and strangers of the earth
Carry their deserts with them, trust no hearth
Not to grow dank with nettles. Some are calm
As hermits with all distance for their home,
Deserts and lonely places filled with light
In which the human plight is cancelled out,
Vision, light's diamond, drawn
Outward towards the rocks struck by the sun,
Splintered upon the quartzite and the snow
And hanging stones frost has not quite let go,
All senses gathered up in the clear air
Absorbed in that transparent fire.

A match lit in the dark, behind the match
A face shows briefly. A latch
Clicks on a door, behind the door
Swiftly the eyes prepare
To be more guarded. A man alone
Is not the figure anyone has known.
In what affections he was whole
All his breaking cannot tell.

A mountain like a shadowy barrier rises.
Beyond lies the defenceless lighted houses
Mile after mile, whose glow spreads on the sky,
And past the town the darkened sea
Rolling beneath the ships on their set courses.
Untrustworthy as chaos the sea's forces,

Details from a Death Certificate

Older than death, support what they destroy,
Support the mind's brief forces that employ
Words like eternity and joy
To say the mind was moved, not understanding,
A creature of the light and dark responding
To light and darkness on earth's dangerous face
And all the quietness of space.

I turn the radio to hear a choir
Blazing fortissimo hosannas. Fire
Of brass instruments excites, but joy
Needing such emphasis hardly rings true;
Richly and splendorously contrived, but doubt
Asks what the singers feel or think about.

Dark chords inhabit harmony, all desiring
Wrung from the knowledge of despairing,
Such harmonies as deaf Beethoven heard,
Not the outpourings of a bird
That in an endless present sings.
Men die in squalor, jerked on strings
Backward or forward as chance takes,
Are cast like skins of snakes,
Yet love, which is entirely human, makes
From the world's elements a conscious light,
Dust of the blind sun burning in its night.

59